Animal Prints

by Charles Broderick
illustrated by Randy Chewning

Practice Decodable 46

McGraw Hill Education

Bothell, WA • Chicago, IL • Columbus, OH • New York, NY

MHEonline.com

Send all inquiries to:
McGraw-Hill Education
8787 Orion Place
Columbus, OH 43240

ISBN: 978-0-02-133312-7
MHID: 0-02-133312-2

Printed in China.

8 9 10 11 12 DSS 27 26 25 24 23

I track animals until dark.

Randal helps.

Where are the animal prints?
Randal and I look for them.

Prints help us track mammals.
I can track a camel!

I see an odd print.
What animal left it?
Is it a fossil?

This animal is different.

It looks as if it had on a sandal.

This is a sandal print.
It is Randal's sandal!